ENDANGERED
MONKEYS

Molly Aloian & Bobbie Kalman

Crabtree Publishing Company

www.crabtreebooks.com

Earth's Endangered Animals Series
A Bobbie Kalman Book

Dedicated by Molly Aloian
For my Grandpa Len, who is far away but still close to my heart

Editor-in-Chief
Bobbie Kalman

Writing team
Molly Aloian
Bobbie Kalman

Substantive editor
Kathryn Smithyman

Editors
Michael Hodge
Robin Johnson
Kelley MacAulay

Photo research
Crystal Foxton

Design
Katherine Kantor
Margaret Amy Salter (cover)

Production coordinator
Heather Fitzpatrick

Consultant
Patricia Loesche, Ph.D., Animal Behavior Program,
Department of Psychology, University of Washington

Illustrations
Barbara Bedell: pages 10, 13 (left)
Margaret Amy Salter: back cover, pages 13 (right), 18, 28

Photographs
© David Lazenby/Animals Animals - Earth Scenes: page 8
ardea.com: Nick Gordon: page 24
Dreamstime.com: © Stefan Ekernas: page 15; © Nick Stubbs: page 19
iStockphoto.com: pages 1, 7, 9 (bottom), 11, 13, 20, 26, 27 (right), 28
Minden Pictures: Claus Meyer: front cover; Mark Moffett: pages 5, 22-23;
    Cyril Ruoso\JH Editorial: pages 27 (left), 29
Naturepl.com: © Anup Shah: page 30; © Adam White: page 25
Photo Researchers, Inc.: Roy Fontaine: page 12
© ShutterStock.com: Steffen Foerster Photography: pages 16, 21;
    Christopher Marin: page 4; Chris Turner: page 31
Visuals Unlimited: Ken Lucas: page 10 (top); Tom Walker: page 17
Other images by Creatas, Digital Vision, and Iconotec

Library and Archives Canada Cataloguing in Publication

Aloian, Molly
    Endangered monkeys / Molly Aloian & Bobbie Kalman.

(Earth's endangered animals)
Includes index.
ISBN 978-0-7787-1862-8 (bound)
ISBN 978-0-7787-1908-3 (pbk.)

    1. Monkeys--Juvenile literature. 2. Endangered species--Juvenile
literature. I. Kalman, Bobbie, 1947- II. Title. III. Series.

QL737.P9A46 2007   j599.8   C2007-900528-4

Library of Congress Cataloging-in-Publication Data

Aloian, Molly.
    Endangered monkeys / Molly Aloian & Bobbie Kalman.
        p. cm. -- (Earth's endangered animals)
    Includes index.
    ISBN-13: 978-0-7787-1862-8 (rlb)
    ISBN-10: 0-7787-1862-X (rlb)
    ISBN-13: 978-0-7787-1908-3 (pb)
    ISBN-10: 0-7787-1908-1 (pb)
    1. Monkeys--Juvenile literature. 2. Endangered species--Juvenile
literature. I. Kalman, Bobbie. II. Title. III. Series.
    QL737.P9A565 2007
    599.8--dc22
                                                2007002693

Crabtree Publishing Company

www.crabtreebooks.com   1-800-387-7650

Published in Canada
Crabtree Publishing
616 Welland Ave.
St. Catharines, ON
L2M 5V6

Published in the United States
Crabtree Publishing
PMB16A
350 Fifth Ave., Suite 3308
New York, NY 10118

Published in the United Kingdom
Crabtree Publishing
White Cross Mills
High Town, Lancaster
LA1 4XS

Published in Australia
Crabtree Publishing
386 Mt. Alexander Rd.
Ascot Vale (Melbourne)
VIC 3032

Contents

Monkeys in danger

Guatemalan black howler monkeys are endangered. Some scientists believe that almost three-quarters of all Guatemalan black howler monkeys will die out in the next 30 years.

Some monkeys are **endangered** animals. Endangered animals are at risk of dying out in the **wild**, or in the natural areas not controlled by people.

Monkeys at risk

In the past, there were several hundred **species**, or types, of monkeys living on Earth. Today, there are only about 165 species of monkeys known to live on Earth. More than 50 of those species are at risk of dying out. People need to help monkeys stay alive or many species may soon become **extinct**.

Words to know

Scientists often use the words listed below to describe animals that are in danger.

vulnerable Describes animals that may soon become endangered

endangered Describes animals that are in danger of dying out in the wild

critically endangered Describes animals that are at high risk of dying out in the wild

extinct Describes animals that are no longer known to live anywhere on Earth

This northern muriqui monkey is critically endangered. Today, there are only about 300 northern muriqui monkeys living in the wild.

What are monkeys?

Monkeys are **mammals**. Mammals are **warm-blooded** animals. The body temperatures of warm-blooded animals stay about the same, no matter how hot or cold their surroundings are. All mammals have **backbones**. Most mammals also have hair or fur on their bodies. Baby mammals **nurse**, or drink milk from the bodies of their mothers.

Primates

Monkeys belong to a group of mammals called **primates**. Primates have larger brains than most other mammals have. All primates have arms, legs, hands, and feet. There are many groups of primates, including lemurs, bush babies, and great apes.

This baby chacma baboon is nursing.

6

Old and new

Most species of monkeys are divided into two main groups—Old World monkeys and New World monkeys. Old World monkeys live in Africa, Asia, and Europe. New World monkeys live in Central America and South America.

Kinds of monkeys

There are more than 80 species of Old World monkeys. Baboons and macaques are examples of Old World monkeys. There are almost 60 species of New World monkeys. Marmosets and squirrel monkeys are examples of New World monkeys.

This olive baboon mother and her baby are Old World monkeys.

This squirrel monkey lives in South America. It is a New World monkey.

7

Where do monkeys live?

Some rainforest monkeys, including this spider monkey, do not come down from the trees. They may never touch the ground during their lives!

Monkeys live in many **habitats**. A habitat is the place in nature where an animal lives. Many species of monkeys live in **tropical rain forests**. Tropical rain forests are hot, dense forests that receive at least 100 inches (254 cm) of rain each year. They are located near the **equator**. The weather near the equator is always hot.

In the trees

New World monkeys live in tropical rain forests in Central America and South America. New World monkeys live high in the branches of trees, where they are hidden from **predators**. Predators are animals that hunt and eat other animals. Large birds and snakes are monkey predators.

More habitats

Old World monkeys live in Africa, Asia, and Europe. Many species of Old World monkeys live in tropical rain forests, but some live in other habitats. Japanese macaques live in cold mountain habitats in northern Japan. Japan is a country in Asia.

Japanese macaques live in forests and on mountains in Japan. Winters are often cold and snowy in the forests and on the mountains.

Savanna monkeys

Some species of Old World monkeys live in Africa on grasslands called **savannas**. Savannas are large areas of flat land that are covered with grasses. Monkeys that live on savannas live mainly on the ground.

Patas monkeys live on grassy savannas in Africa.

9

Monkey bodies

A mandrill's head is very large. This monkey has a yellow beard and red patches of fur above its eyes.

Monkeys have fur covering their bodies. Some species have long fur, and other species have short fur. Some species have fur that is just one color. The fur of other monkey species is **multicolored**, or more than one color.

Small or big

Some monkeys have small bodies. Others have large bodies. The pygmy marmoset is the smallest monkey. It is only about 15 inches (38 cm) long and weighs 7 ounces (198 g). The mandrill is the biggest monkey. A male mandrill can be almost three feet (1 m) long and weigh over 100 pounds (45 kg)!

Fingers and toes

Monkeys have fingers on their hands and toes on their feet. They use their fingers and toes to pick up and hold objects. Some monkeys also have thumbs. All monkeys have nails on their fingers and toes. They use their nails to help them pick up small objects.

Monkey have muscular bodies. Their bodies are **agile**, or able to move quickly and easily.

Some monkeys have long, **flexible** tails. Their tails are sometimes longer than the rest of their bodies are!

Monkeys have long, slender arms and legs. They use their arms and legs to run, walk, and climb trees. They also use them to swing from branch to branch.

Monkeys have strong, flexible hands and feet. They grip branches and hold food and other objects with them.

11

More about monkey bodies

New World monkeys, including this red spider monkey, often use their tails as extra legs or arms.

The bodies of Old World monkeys are different from the bodies of New World monkeys. For example, New World monkeys have long, flexible, **prehensile** tails. Prehensile body parts are able to grasp. New World monkeys can hold objects with their tails.

A tale of tails

Old World monkeys do not have prehensile tails. Their tails are often short. Old World monkeys use their tails for balance while they leap through trees. Other differences between the bodies of Old World monkeys and New World monkeys are shown on the next page.

12

Old World monkeys

- Old World monkeys have nostrils that point downward.

- Old World monkeys have tough pads of skin on their bottoms.

- Old World monkeys have thumbs that are **opposable**. An opposable thumb can move toward and touch the fingers on the same hand. Old World monkeys can use their thumbs to help them hold objects.

New World monkeys

- New World monkeys have nostrils that point sideways.

- New World monkeys do not have pads of skin on their bottoms.

- New World monkeys do not have opposable thumbs. Some species have very small thumbs. Others have no thumbs at all. They have only fingers. New World monkeys cannot use their thumbs to hold objects.

13

Living together

Monkeys live in groups called **troups**. Some troups are small. A small troup is made up of a **mature**, or an adult, male monkey and a mature female monkey. Other troups are large. There can be up to 500 monkeys in a large troup! A large troup is made up of mature male and female monkeys and young male and female monkeys. Older monkeys in the troup help care for and protect the young monkeys. Young monkeys learn how to climb trees and find food and water by watching the older monkeys in their troup.

The monkeys in a troup work together to find food and to protect one another from predators. This picture shows a baboon troup.

In charge

In some troups, one or a few adult male monkeys are **dominant**. Dominant monkeys are in charge of the other monkeys in their troups. They are the biggest and strongest males. Dominant monkeys decide where the troups eat and sleep at night. In some monkey species, adult females are the dominant monkeys in their troups. Marmosets have dominant females.

This large male baboon is a dominant monkey.

Troup territories

Many monkey troups have **territories**. A territory is the area in which a troup lives, finds food, and rests. Troups that live in habitats with plenty of food have small territories. In tropical rain forests, for example, troups can find enough food to eat in a small area. Some monkey troups live in habitats where food is harder to find, such as on savannas. Troups living on savannas have large territories. They must travel long distances to find enough food to eat.

15

Monkey messages

Monkeys **communicate**, or send messages to one another, in different ways. Some monkeys make sounds to call to one another. They bark, grunt, roar, and click. They use these sounds as warnings that other monkeys are entering their territories. They also make sounds to scare away predators from their troups.

*Monkeys use **facial expressions** to communicate with one another. An **aggressive** monkey may open its mouth and show its teeth.*

Body talk

A monkey also communicates by moving its body in certain ways. An angry monkey may shake tree branches or jump up and down. It may also stare directly at its enemy. If a monkey feels comfortable with another monkey, the two monkeys will huddle close to one another.

Making friends

Monkeys **groom**, or clean, themselves every day. The members of a troup also groom one another. Grooming is another way monkeys communicate. It is a way for monkeys to show affection and to make friends with other monkeys in their troups.

This monkey is using its nails to scratch and pick at another monkey's fur. It is picking out dirt, dead skin, and parasites.

17

A monkey's life cycle

Every animal goes through a set of changes from the time it is born to the time it is an adult. This set of changes is called a **life cycle**. A monkey's life cycle begins when it is born. The newborn monkey is tiny. It stays very close to its mother.

The young monkey grows and changes until it is mature. A mature monkey can **mate**, or join together with another monkey of the same species to make babies. Each time a baby monkey is born, a new life cycle begins.

The life cycle of a squirrel monkey

A newborn squirrel monkey weighs about four ounces (113 g). It begins to nurse right after it is born.

A female squirrel monkey is mature at two-and-a-half years of age. A male squirrel monkey is mature at two-and-a-half to four years of age. An adult squirrel monkey can live to be up to fifteen years old.

The baby clings to its mother's back for several weeks. It continues to nurse. After about six months, it stops nursing and starts eating fruit, leaves, and some insects.

Growing up

A mother monkey carries her baby with her, either on her back or against her chest. The baby monkey stays close to its mother and nurses. Most baby monkeys nurse for between six and fifteen months. The baby monkey's body becomes bigger and stronger as it nurses. When the baby is strong enough, its mother begins to teach it how to find food and avoid predators. After about one year, the young monkey can survive on its own.

Getting along

A mother monkey encourages her baby to get along with other members of its troup. Other mature females in the troup often help the mother monkey raise her baby. They protect the young monkey and bring it food to eat.

A newborn monkey is tiny and helpless. It needs its mother to stay alive.

Monkey food

Some monkeys are **herbivores**. Herbivores are animals that eat only plants. Black howler monkeys are herbivores. They eat leaves, fruits, **buds**, and flowers. Many monkey herbivores eat only leaves. Animals that eat only leaves are called **folivores**.

Food for omnivores

Other monkeys are **omnivores**. Omnivores are animals that eat both plants and animals. Monkeys that are omnivores eat any foods they can find. Mandrills and baboons are omnivores. They eat fruits, seeds, roots, **forbs**, worms, frogs, insects, snails, and lizards.

Monkeys have back teeth called **molars**. *They use their molars to grind leaves and fruit into mush. They then swallow this food.*

20

Being cheeky

Some species of Old World monkeys, such as this Sykes monkey, have pockets on the insides of their cheeks. The pockets are called **cheek pouches**. Monkeys fill their cheek pouches with food and store the food to eat later. The cheek pouches of some Old World monkeys are quite large. They start at the lower teeth and stretch down to the monkeys' necks. New World monkeys do not have cheek pouches.

cheek pouch

21

Habitat loss

One of the greatest threats to monkeys is **habitat loss**. Habitat loss is the destruction of the natural areas in which animals live and find food. Each year, the number of people on Earth increases. People need more and more space for homes, businesses, and roads. As a result, they are taking over the habitats of many animals, including monkeys.

Cleared out

People **clear** large areas of monkey habitats. To clear means to remove the trees and other plants from an area. People are clearing some parts of tropical rain forests to make space for cattle to **graze**. They clear other parts of tropical rain forests to make room for roads, villages, and **crops**. Crops are plants that are grown for food. This tropical rain forest was cleared so people could grow coffee beans in its place.

Nothing to eat

Many monkey species live and find food high in tropical rainforest trees. For example, colobus monkeys live in trees and eat mainly leaves that grow on the trees. When people cut down rainforest trees, monkeys lose their habitats and supply of food. With nowhere to live or find food, many monkey species cannot survive.

Hunting monkeys

*Some people in Africa eat monkey meat. The meat of wild African animals is sometimes called **bushmeat**. This woman is drying monkey meat, which she will later sell as bushmeat.*

People hunt and kill monkeys. They hunt monkeys even when it is **illegal**, or against the law, to do so. People kill monkeys and then sell their meat, bones, fur, **organs**, brains, and other body parts for money.

Monkey meat

People sometimes **smuggle** monkey body parts into countries in Asia and Europe. To smuggle means to move something into or out of a country illegally. In European and Asian countries, some restaurants serve foods that contain monkey body parts and charge high prices for them. In China, monkey brains are a **delicacy**.

Almost extinct

The Delacour's langur is a critically endangered monkey species that lives in Vietnam. People continue to hunt and kill these monkeys, however. They kill the monkeys for their meat. People also sell the bones, organs, and other body parts of the monkeys. Many scientists believe that if people continue to kill Delacour's langurs, these animals will soon become extinct.

Capturing and training

Some people **capture** baby monkeys in the wild and sell them as pets. Pet monkeys are sold for thousands of dollars. Monkeys should never be kept as pets, however. Baby monkeys may look very small and cute.

When baby monkeys grow up, they can be dangerous. As adults, monkeys often become aggressive toward their owners. To be healthy and happy, monkeys need to live in the wild and be around other monkeys.

Many people sell or give away their pet monkeys, once they realize how difficult monkeys are to keep as pets. The monkeys may eventually end up living in small zoos. People who work at these zoos may not be able to care for the monkeys properly.

Working monkeys

In Malaysia, some people train macaques to climb to the tops of palm trees, pick coconuts, and bring them down to their owners. The owners then sell the coconuts. A macaque can pick many more coconuts in a day than a person can. The animals are often punished if they do not behave well, however.

This pig-tailed macaque is picking coconuts for its owner. Pig-tailed macaques are a vulnerable monkey species.

Trained to do tricks

In certain parts of Asia, people own monkeys and train them to perform tricks. The monkeys earn money for their owners because people pay money to watch the tricks. The owners are often cruel to their monkeys. They keep the monkeys on short, tight leashes or in small cages. They may even hit the animals or yell at them when the monkeys do not do as they are told.

Protecting monkeys

The governments of many countries protect the areas in which monkeys live. Many people around the world are also working hard to protect monkeys. People who work to protect monkeys and other animals often form **conservation groups**. Conservation International is one such group. Members of conservation groups teach business owners and farmers how to grow crops without destroying the habitats of monkeys and other animals.

Some conservation groups work hard to make sure that people who buy and sell monkeys are punished.

28

Breeding monkeys

Some people **breed** endangered monkeys. To breed means to cause animals of the same species to mate and have babies in **captivity**. People breed endangered monkeys in safe places called **sanctuaries**. In sanctuaries, the monkeys are protected from habitat loss, hunters, and other threats. The babies born in sanctuaries grow into mature monkeys and have babies of their own. Some of the monkeys are then released into the wild. Other monkeys stay in the sanctuaries. As more endangered monkeys have babies in sanctuaries, the **populations** of endangered monkeys grows bigger. The mandrills in the picture above live at the Pandrillus, Drill Rehabilitation and Breeding Center in Nigeria. The center was created in 1991.

Learning more

*This woman is a **primatologist**. A primatologist is a person who studies primates. This primatologist is studying mother and baby patas monkeys.*

There is a lot to learn about monkeys! Some scientists study monkeys in the wild. They study what monkeys eat and how often they **reproduce**, or have babies. Scientists also study monkeys in their troups. They count troup members, and observe how the monkeys behave and communicate with one another.

Protecting monkeys

Studying monkeys is a great way to help these animals. By learning about what monkeys need in order to stay alive, scientists can protect monkeys in their habitats.

Learn and share

Monkeys may live far from you, but you can still learn about them and help them! Visit your local library and read other books about monkeys. Watch television programs about monkeys, too. The Internet is another great place to find information about monkeys. Share everything you learn with your friends, teachers, and family. The more information people know about monkeys, the more they will want to protect these animals. Visit the websites below and learn as much as you can about monkeys and other primates!

- www.enchantedlearning.com/ subjects/mammals/monkey/ Monkeyprintout.shtml

- anthro.palomar.edu/primate/ prim_4.htm

- www.primates.com/welcome.htm

Read books and search the Internet to learn about this cotton-top tamarin. Is it a New World monkey or an Old World Monkey? What foods does it eat? Is it a fast climber?

Glossary

Note: Boldfaced words that are defined in the text may not appear in the glossary.

aggressive Describing the behavior of an animal that is angry or ready to attack

backbone A row of bones in the middle of an animal's back

bud A small part on a plant, which will grow into a leaf or a flower

captivity A state of living in an enclosed area such as a zoo

capture To take something by force

conservation group An organization of people who work to protect and save living things

delicacy An expensive and fancy food

equator An imaginary line around the center of Earth

facial expression A look on the face of an animal that shows how the animal is feeling

flexible Describing something that can bend easily

forb A type of flowering plant

graze To feed on grass

organ A part of the body, such as the heart or liver, which does an important job

parasite A living thing that lives on or inside another living thing

population The total number of one species of animal living in an area

sanctuary A reserved area of land in which animals are protected from hunting and other dangers

Index

Printed in the U.S.A.